Real Estate: Learn to Succeed the First Time

Real Estate Basics, Home Buying, Real Estate Investment and House Flipping

2nd Edition

Table of Contents

Introduction

I was once asked how I got into the real estate business and it was quite a hard question to answer. In my case, it was necessity. Having very little money to invest in real estate, but being a very practical minded person, I was able to purchase houses at relatively low prices and make sense of the market, so that I could sell these on and make a handsome profit. What I learned on the journey was very interesting. It isn't just a case of speculating to accumulate. You do need to know what you are looking for and you also need to know what it will cost you to make the home that you have bought fit a specific market.

You also need to learn when to walk away and that's the hard point that some people who invest in real estate don't watch for. This can be the difference between making money and losing your investment. In this book, I will use my personal experience to explain how you can make your experience as a home buyer or as a potential house flipper successful. You will learn all about buying houses at bargain prices, about the study that you need to put into the market, and how this study pays off long term.

It isn't as simple as buying a house and doing it up. The real estate industry is much more complex than that. You have to bear in mind the state of the market, the area of the market that you are competing in, the cost of refurbishment and the overall length of time that you will have your money tied up in property. With the right attitude and the right way of approaching the real estate market, it can be a very profitable and worthwhile way to make money. Without the expertise and without taking precautions, it can be a disaster. This book will help you to understand how it all works and what you can do to ensure that your real estate gives you the best return. You will learn all about what to look for in a new property so that you avoid some of the more common the pitfalls.

Chapter 1 – Real Estate Basics

Before we get started, let's establish some basic real estate terms. If you currently do not own a home and are looking to purchase your first piece of real estate, you are a potential buyer. In most cases, potential buyers work with banks to enter a standard mortgage, which I will explain later. The bank that gives you or originates your mortgage is the lender, and you are the borrower and the home buyer. The person or entity that you purchase the home from is the seller. Once the papers are signed saying you are paying a mortgage for a property, you are now the homeowner.

You enter the real estate marketplace the moment that you buy your first home. It is important to think about the location and the cost before making the decision to invest in real estate. To purchase that house, you need to know the area you're buying in and have set your finances up to be able to pay your current bills as well as any bills that are incurred at the new location.

Setting a budget will be discussed in Chapter Two. Creating a financial plan is the first step to determining your real estate abilities. A financial plan will help you determine what sort of borrowing ability you have and what your credit needs are.

Buying your first house? Homeownership brings many benefits. One of the benefits is that you're able to take control of your housing instead of living in an apartment complex which may raise their rent every year. In comparison, your mortgage will remain the same over an extended period. Apartments often do not allow residents to make drastic changes to the rental unit. When you own your home, you can have it meet your needs and tastes.

Homeownership also builds home equity. Your assets will grow with the principal portion of your mortgage payments as your property value potentially increases. Additionally, you can deduct mortgage interest and real estate property taxes on your income tax. By making on-time, monthly mortgage payments, you will also build your credit.

While the benefits of homeownership are significant, you have to decide if you are ready for a serious and long-term commitment. It is said that with freedom comes responsibility. Homeowners are responsible for all utilities, maintenance, and repairs, in addition to mortgage payments, property taxes, and homeowners insurance. There may also be homeowner association (HOA) fees. Also, unlike an apartment, in a year, you can't pick up and leave. Before moving on from your house, there are more complicated steps to take.

When you purchase a house, you will likely work with a bank or another lender to provide the upfront funding of the full cost of your house. Your upfront contribution includes a down payment and closing costs. Down payments are applied to the principle balance of the house and lower your loan amount. For example, if you purchase a home for $300,000 and put $25,000 down, your loan will only be for $275,000. The higher your down payment, the lower your monthly mortgage payments will be.

There are many different types of mortgages available for you to choose. Below we will highlight the different options.

Most people do not have the ability to own a home without a mortgage. Mortgage payments generally have four parts: principle, interest, taxes, and insurance. The principle is the balance of your mortgage. In our example above, that would be $275,000. Interest is the cost paid to the lender. An interest rate is the percentage of your loan amount that is charged to borrow money, and is based on current market conditions, credit scores, down payments and the type of mortgage you choose. Taxes are charged and paid to your local government. Insurance is collected and paid to an escrow account to protect you from loss or damage to any property. Escrow is a holding account for funds, typically kept by a third-party who can only be used if certain conditions are met. Conditions could include extensive home repairs, property taxes, and homeowners insurance. In many states, escrow and title insurance, which we'll discuss later, are held by the same party. Depending on your loan term, the amount of time you have to pay off your balance, your monthly payment may be higher or lower. The longer the loan term, the lower the mortgage payment.

The most straightforward mortgage option available is a fixed-rate mortgage. With this option, home buyers pay a fixed interest rate on the loan for a fixed amount of time, typically 30 years. The monthly mortgage payment does not change throughout the life of the loan. The majority of early payments go toward interest while the bulk of later payments go toward the principal balance. However, with an interest-only fixed-rate mortgage, you will only pay interest for an initial period, established based on the terms of your agreement. After this initial period, the loan will be adjusted and include interest and principal in the monthly payment. This model is called a hybrid adjustable-rate mortgage (ARM).

Also known as a variable-rate mortgage, an ARM determines the interest rate according to a benchmark. In most agreements, the initial interest rate is fixed for a period, then readjusted in specific intervals. For example, a home buyer may pay an initial fixed interest rate for two years and then pays a floating rate for the remaining 23 years of the 25-year mortgage.

Another option is an interest-only mortgage. You enter this type of mortgage for a certain amount of time, and all monthly payments cover interest. In this case, you do not own any parts of the house; however, at the end of your interest-only term, you have the option to enter a standard fixed-rate or adjustable rate mortgage. Interest-only mortgages tend to cost home buyers much more than standard mortgages. However, this is an option for someone who prefers to have low monthly costs for a shorter period of time and plans to make more money in the future.

For low-income individuals and veterans, there are government programs available to help fund a mortgage. Federal Housing Administration (FHA) grants mortgage loans with a lower down payment to help low-income individuals pay for mortgage insurance. These loans are given out by FHA-insured lenders. FHA insured loans may include closing and legal costs. Provided by the Department of Veterans Affairs, Veterans Affairs (VA) mortgage loans are available to veterans and active military members. VA loans do not always require a down payment or mortgage insurance. There is also no minimum credit score required; however, lenders may have their own requirements.

Reverse mortgages are an option for current homeowners. You can access the equity in the home by receiving a lump-sum payment or monthly cash payments. This type of mortgage is typically only available to homeowners who are at least 62 years old, live in the home and are close to paying or already have paid off their mortgage. In a nutshell, reverse mortgages provide tax-free cash to homeowners.

While you may enter a mortgage with initial financing for your home, you have the opportunity to refinance. Refinancing is acquiring a new loan to replace an existing one. Homeowners take advantage of refinancing to have a loan with better terms. Refinancing can save homeowners thousands of dollars; however, it can also be more expensive. Sometimes low introductory rates on adjustable-rate mortgages may sway a homeowner to refinance, but the higher rate it reaches could be very costly.

During the time that you own the property, whether you are buying it to flip or to live in, you are responsible for the utilities and all taxes related to that house. Make sure you look around the market before buying. You want to have a comparison before making an offer. That means that you can weigh up one investment against another. Some people with less money to invest may choose to opt for a house that needs repairs over a longer period of time. The fact that the house is in a bad state of repair will mean that the price on the market will have been relatively lower but the trick is working out what the home would be worth once all of these repairs are done and what the cost of those repairs is likely to come to. Additionally, rates will vary on home loans. If you're a member of the military, VA loans may be your best option, however, you should look at the terms of that agreement in comparison to other institutions. Also, credit unions may offer better terms that a bank or other lender. A good rule of thumb is to speak with at least three different lenders to see what your best deal will be.

Equity is the amount of money that a property gives you as the potential for another loan on a property. If your property was bought for $100,000 and is currently worth $150,000, then you have an equity of $50,000 or you may find that your lender would be happy to advance that amount, depending upon how convinced the lender is that the value of the property would be reached should you default on your payments.

Another consideration when buying a home is the neighborhood. Fair Housing Laws were created to protect classes of race, color, national origin, religious preference, sex, familial status and handicaps. As a buyer, you are protected from public entities funneling homebuyers to a particular area in order to maintain or change the makeup of a neighborhood. Therefore, anyone selling a home is unable to make claims about the neighborhood. For example, if you were to ask a real estate agent if there are a lot of business professionals in the area, she or he could not answer. What this law also does is insure everyone has a right to sell, buy, lease or rent housing properties, regardless of their race, color, religion, sex, handicap, familial status, or national origin.

There are different scales that you need to remember as well. The market value may differ from a valuation of the home for bank purposes because all a bank wants to know is if they will get their money back. The market value, however, may be something that is flexible depending upon changes in the market. For example, if there are not many houses for sale, then the house is more valuable because it's a rarity and something that people will be looking for. If there is a housing surplus and there are too many choices, then it is likely that it's a buyer's market and you may get less for your house. The other valuation you need to keep in mind is the valuation for insurance purposes is totally different from the previous types of valuation. This should be based on what it would cost you to replace the house in the event of it being destroyed. An insurance company will be able to give you a valuation so that you know what insurance is likely to cost you.

Do not count out foreclosed properties when looking to purchase a home. Houses get foreclosed on when the previous owner defaults on the loan. Foreclosed homes tend to be more affordable, but finalizing your transaction can be a much longer process. In some cases, the seller isn't concerned with making a profit and simply wants to be free of the property. Foreclosed properties are sold in as-is condition. There are different ways of obtaining a foreclosed property; however, the ability to negotiate will vary based on the sale type.

Current homeowners still have control of a property during pre-foreclosure, however, in order to avoid defaulting on the loan, the homeowner has negotiated to sell the house below market value, known as a short sale. In real estate, you have different types of sales. Short sales are when you can buy a property at less than the amount that the seller owes to the bank. In a case like this, the bank may have given up on ever getting back the amount owed and may agree that the seller can sell to pay off as much as the house is likely to realize. The problem with short sale prices is that they don't always turn out to be as wonderful of a house as the purchasers think it will be. There may be repairs needed that are excessive, but purchasers jump in blindly because they feel like they are getting a great bargain. A home inspection costs money, but it doesn't cost as much as the potential loss that you can make if you buy a short sale property that needs more care than its worth.

After signing the short sale agreement, the seller will vacate the property. Short sale properties tend to have a higher value because the owners are ahead of the financial problems with the home. Short sale homes are sold as-is, but the buyer can ask to inspect the property.

Property owners can also refuse a short sale. In this case, or if the owner is unable to sell during pre-foreclosure, the house moves into foreclosure and is sold at auction.

Auction properties – these are usually properties which have been foreclosed on. The existing owner cannot afford to pay the mortgage and the bank wants back the money that is owed. Now these can be a real bargain if you know what damage needs repairing and you are aware of the market. We will go into this later, but basically these are houses the bank is prepared to sell for the amount owed on a specific date. The advantage of these sales is that you can get bargains. The disadvantage is that you need to have inspected the property in a short space of time and should have the financing in place before you bid. The mistake that people make with this kind of purchase is that they bid above their budget and leave less money for repairs.

There are two types of auctions: a public foreclosure auction or a public auction through an auction company. Conducted by a neutral third party, at a public foreclosure auction, you have the opportunity to be the highest bidder and pay with cash for a foreclosed property. It's common for bidders not to have the right to view or inspect an auctioned property. Before purchasing a home through auction, investigate any liens or encumbrances on the home. On the other hand, properties that have not successfully sold after an extended period of time may be outsourced to an auction company.

If the property isn't sold at auction, it will move into full possession of the lender, known as real-estate owned (REO). These properties are the most popular; the process for purchasing is easy and safe, but offers little to no room for negotiation. Lenders tend to clear any items from the home and clean the house for sale. They will also clear any liens on the property. Another bonus is an FHA 203(k) Renovation Loan, available for repairs on real-estate owned purchased to fund the "as improved" value of a house.

If purchasing a foreclosed home is for you, begin your search. You'll be able to find many foreclosed homes listed for sale the same way as traditional homes. You can start your search with online real estate listings and websites, as well as the newspapers. Various bank websites may also list real-estate owned properties that are available for sale. If a property is moved to an auction company, the company will host and market an auction either in-person or online.

Sales through real estate agent - These are houses that have been put on the market for a variety of reasons. Perhaps the owners are moving to a new town. Perhaps they are simply moving to a larger home. In the case of seniors, these seniors may be moving into assisted living and don't need a large home any more. There can be all kinds of reasons a house comes onto the market. The advantage of this kind of sale is that you can usually find out the background of the house and have more time in which to investigate and decide upon the value of the home. You also have more bargaining power because the real estate agent will act as a liaison between you and the seller.

For a rental investment, the disadvantage is that it ties up your initial money and unless you have more money for your next investment, this may not be a good move. However, if you have excess cash to invest, you may find that you will be able to recoup any mortgage payments from tenants which means that the investment pays for itself over a period of time.

Before making any offers, regardless of the purchase process, you should have a professional inspection performed on the home. Inspections protect you and potentially save you money in the long run. Inspections will determine the current condition of the home, the estimated cost of repairs, and a fair and reasonable offer. Although the upfront work appears to be arduous, it can result in a true bargain. When in doubt, consult a qualified professional and do your research to make the best decision for you.

Another way of obtaining property is through a probate sale. When someone dies without bequeathing their property to anyone, the home is sold in probate court. Properties sold in probate court typically take longer than traditional real estate sales. The state is the administrator of probate sales. The lengthy process is due to assessments and procedures that are required by the court to ensure property is sold at the best possible price. Probate attorneys will hire a real estate agent, sign a listing agreement, and show the property like with traditional listings. Price is based on the home's appraisal coupled with the real estate agent's suggestions.

Potential buyers can make an offer at any time, but must pay a 10% deposit. In most cases, the deposit is non-refundable. The probate attorney can accept, counter or decline the offer. If accepted, the offer must be confirmed by the court. If the original buyer isn't the final buyer, it may be refunded, but is not guaranteed. The probate attorney will petition the court for a date to confirm the sale. Once the date is determined, the court and potential buyer must wait a minimum of 30 to 45 days to ensure the home is selling for the best possible price. This is confirmed by advertising the property for a higher price during the wait period. On the date of sale, the property is auctioned. If multiple buyers bid, the highest bidder wins and they must immediately pay a 10% deposit. If no one but the original potential buyer shows, then the property is sold at the original offer price.

There are a lot of steps to obtaining property through probate sales, but you can have the property inspected before making an offer. Although you could potentially lose the money you use for an inspection, you will know if waiting for the home is worth it. Probate sales are risky because the owner is deceased and can't disclose any issues with the home. Take matters into your own hands before spending thousands of dollars by inspecting the property.

Once you own your first property, you can choose to live in it or flip it. Flipping a house is when the property owner either buys a house at low value and sells it for a much higher value, or buys a house that needs repairs, fixes it up to increase its value and resells it for a profit. You will be responsible for utilities and taxes on a home whether you buy it to flip or live. House flipping will be discussed in a later chapter.

Flipping houses is just one of many real estate investment strategies. This book will teach you the basics on real estate while also equipping you with the knowledge you need to go out and start investing like a pro! If you are not ready to dive head first into real estate investing, it is okay to start small. There are investment options that do not require huge time and financial commitments. But first, let's go over some additional basic real estate investing lingo.

Appreciation is an increase in the value of your property over time. Property can appreciate if the demand for real estate increases, or as a result of inflation or changes in interest rates. In contrast, a property's value may decrease in value. Often a result of unfavorable market conditions, this decrease is called depreciation.

Depreciation is also the process of deducting costs of buying and improving rental properties. When you invest in a property, there are some tax benefits. You could take one large tax deduction in the year you purchase or improve the property, or you can deduct depreciation, which is the value of the property over its useful lifetime. Tax benefits of real estate will be discussed in a later chapter.

Cash flow is the net amount of cash moving in and out of a business. Your goal is always to have a positive cash flow, which means you have more money coming in than you are paying out. The difference between how much you make and how much you need to pay is your profit.

Another key term is leverage. You are leveraging when you use borrowed capital to purchase property. The expectation is that the profits you earn from the investment will be greater than the interest payable on the borrowed monies.

You enter real estate investing to make a profit. A good way to keep track of this profit is through return on investment or ROI. ROI is a metric used to evaluate profitability by subtracting your investment amount, which includes loan and down payment, from your net income, then dividing by your investment amount. For example, if you invest $110,000, and you made a profit of $20,000, then your net income is $130,000 minus $110,000 divided by $110,000 for an 18% return on investment.

Chapter 2 – Deciding on Your Budget

When you enter the real estate market, you need to know how much you can afford to spend. This should include the cost of the home as well as the legal fees, agent's fees, sufficient money to renovate the house as needed and put it back onto the market. During the time that you own the house, it will gain no income and will be a liability. Therefore, your budget must include a fixed period of time where you will be expected to pay the mortgage while any work needed is being completed. People often forget about this aspect of cost but every month that you own the house will cost you money and should be counted.

When you apply for a loan, banks will look at a number of areas as the main criteria for their decision.

Is your income source reliable? Banks want to know that based on your income, you are able to make on-time, monthly payments. Income can come from primary, secondary, or part-time employment, overtime, commission, bonuses, veteran's benefits, rental income, and more. Banks will look back over a significant length of time to ensure your income is stable.

What is your credit history? Your payment habits will be a deciding factor in loan offers. Banks want to ensure that you have a history of paying back your debts. Banks will also look at your current debts to determine if an additional loan is suitable for you. What is the property market value? Before making anything official, banks will order a property appraisal to ensure the value of the property is comparable to what the bank will pay.

Do you have enough funds for a down payment? Not only do future homeowners have to pay a down payment, but there are also closing costs associated with purchasing a home.

You must have funds available to cover these. Funds can come from multiple sources. You also need to show that you can cover several months of mortgage payments.

Do you make enough to cover all your debts? This is called a debt-to-income ratio. Banks will evaluate the percentage of your monthly income that is spent on debts. If the percentage is too high, this will factor into the decision on your loan application. Banks will also evaluate your new housing expenses to ensure you can cover your new debts.

When you are deciding upon your budget, bear in mind what the bank is prepared to offer you and what this will cost you during the time that you own the property. You also need to ensure that you can afford home owners insurance for the period that you own the property and know what taxes apply to your ownership.

Many mortgage lenders require at least 20% of the value of the house down in order to buy property. In reality, many people do not have that money easily available to them. However, there are strategies for investing little to no money on a property. We've discussed owner-occupant agreements and house hacking as a potential way of saving on upfront costs. Another strategy is finding private and hard money.

Hard money lending is a risky, yet available option for a low down payment. Upfront, hard money can be used instead of your own cash. However, be aware that interest rates and fees on hard money is much higher than conventional loans. Hard money is arranged by brokers, who typically pair a private investor with a borrower. Brokers serve as an intermediary and will work with individuals who need cash quickly, making this strategy most suitable for someone flipping houses. Hard money loans are short-term and determined by the ARV. Lenders will loan up to 75% ARV on the property and also assess points on your loan. Points are a fee equal to 1% of your loan amount. As opposed to other loans, you do not make monthly payments on hard money. Instead, you pay a lump sum for the loan principle and interest at the time of sale.

There are three types of borrowers that typically take out hard money loans: rural buyers, buyers of expensive properties, and borrowers at risk of foreclosure. Traditional lenders are hesitant to loan to rural buyers because the property derives a substantial portion of its value from the land rather than the home. Thus, rural buyers turn to hard money loans to cover the full costs. Borrowers at risk of foreclosure turn to hard money loans on rainy days. If a borrower is behind, they may take out a hard money loan to catch them up and avoid their home going into foreclosure. Buyers of expensive properties have the ability to turn around and make large profits on a property; however, there can be downfalls. Buyers do like the lack of red tape and restrictions that come with a hard money loan also. You make your money with hard money if 75% of your new appraisal after the repairs are done, is greater than your hard money loan amount. The risk you run is your appraisal coming out lower than you expect. Let's put numbers with this strategy.

You want to buy an $80,000 house with a $150,000 ARV. The lender agrees to loan 75% ARV on the property. Your hard money loan will be for $112,500. If the lender charges 18% interest and five points, then you will pay $10,125 in interest and $5,625 for points. In order to make a profit, you would need a new appraisal of at least $128,250.

As you can see, hard money loans can add up quickly. You must pay off your hard money loan at the end of the term and you will want to have an exit strategy if the appraisal isn't as high as it needs to be.

One way of avoiding the costs of hard money loans is to find a partner. Partners help alleviate the financial burden of real estate investing. Perhaps you already know someone who is involved with investments. Pitch your real estate plan and ask for him or her to partner with you. Your partnership could be as simple as your partner financing the investment and you doing all of the work, but splitting profits 50-50. If you find the right partner, you can build your reputation for little money and build your profits.

While hard money loans act as a middle man for private lenders, you also have the option of going out finding your own private money lender. You will want to offer high enough interest that lending to you is worth it to the lender. You could ask them what kind of return they're looking for in their investment. Whatever rate they are looking for, you will want to insure that you can still make a profit by taking out the loan.

You must have a definite cap on what you can afford to spend because this allows you to only look at houses which fall into your price range and a little higher, bearing in mind that there is always room for negotiation. It helps to be able to get a contractor to give you initial quotes on the cost to do any repairs on the property. Remodeling can be expensive but necessary to raise the value of the home or to repair items in the home that need to be in good working order. Depending on the work that needs to be done, you may need to consult with plumbers, electricians, or just general contractors to get the best quotes and ideas for renovations.

I would say to anyone who wants to get into this business that you need to be fairly aware of what average repairs cost. For example, I have a list of current costs that I refer to when looking at new properties:

The cost of rewiring a basic three bedroomed house

The cost of rewiring a two bedroomed apartment

The cost of installing a kitchen into X amount of square feet

The cost of replacing guttering

The cost of replacing slipped shingle or tile

The cost of installing a subfloor over X amount of square feet

The cost of removing asbestos

The cost of getting rid of mold over a set amount of square feet

Before you even think of stepping foot into a house, have a folder put together with realistic costs that are hypothetical but which give you an idea of what you are looking at. The kinds of jobs that you will be able to use unskilled labor for are the initial ripping out of old items from the property and making it ready for contractors. You will need to know what day rate someone charges because often this kind of work is done on a day rate. However, be careful. Make sure that your idea of a day is the same as theirs.

Other costs that will come into the picture are things such as dumpsters. In the initial stages of ownership these will save you a lot of time and you need to know of a local company who can deliver one on a fast turnaround and remove it when you need it and the cost for such work.

Other ways that you can cut down on your budget is to set up accounts at your local stores so that you are eligible for discounts for supplies, lumber, fixtures, and other renovation needs. This will help you to save money. Builder's stores that sell dry wall and all of the items needed for the refurbishment should be able to offer you a credit account. This allows you to budget for the expenses rather than have sticker shock at the cost of supplies per trip.

Be informed. Pre-qualification and preapproval are two different services that mortgage lenders may provide. Pre-qualification is a general estimate of the loan amount you may qualify for based on preliminary information. A credit report is not pulled for pre-qualification. On the other hand, preapproval requires a submitted loan application and credit check. With preapproval, you know the approximate mortgage loan amount and purchase price range you qualify for, subject to conditions or documentation. Preapproval gives bidders maximum leverage and shows sellers that you are a serious buyer. When negotiating, pre-approval provides you with negotiating strength, as you are well-informed on your budget.

You may find that some improvements to houses will be eligible for grants and you need to be aware of this since working within the guidelines given can save you a lot of money. Find out if this only applies to your principal residence or whether grants are available for houses that you intend to sell. You also need to know from an accountant or someone who is qualified to tell you what capital gains tax applies to houses. These rules will help you to work out what you budget is and what you are likely to make from a house.

Any home loan that is worth more than 80% of the value of the home requires home buyers have private mortgage insurance (PMI), which will pay some or all of the loan balance if the homeowner is unable to make mortgage payments. If you are unable to pay 20% of the value of the home towards the down payment, then you are subject to this additional bill. However, there is a way to avoid it. You are able to have a second mortgage. You can take out a primary loan to cover the majority of the value of the home, make your down payment, and take out a second mortgage to cover the difference. It is up to you to figure out what is the better option for you.

Taxes

Local governments make a nice chunk of change off personal property taxes. As discussed earlier, when you own a home, a portion of your mortgage payment will go towards taxes. The rules and rates vary by state and location. Also, depending on the type of property you have, you may be subject to additional taxes. For example, a home that uses well water may have to pay a severance tax.

In most cases, taxes are calculated and assessed based on the fair market value (FMV) of the home. The value is multiplied by a ratio to determine a portion that will be taxed at the appropriate tax rate. It's important to note that the value of property changes over time and it is required to have your home revalued every three or four years.

Taxes can become costly, but fortunately, there are deductions and other incentives that can help reduce your tax bill. By itemizing on certain line items of your tax forms, you will see a difference in your bill. Tax breaks include mortgage interest, real estate taxes, energy credits, home equity loans, and mortgage insurance premiums.

Mortgage interest is the biggest tax break for most homeowners. You can deduct any interest paid on your interest on debt up to $1 million. The amount for the previous year will be listed on your Form 1098, which is sent by your lender by January 31. Be sure to keep track of what you are paying. Even if how much you paid isn't listed on the Form 1098, you can still deduct it.

You can also deduct those hefty local property taxes we just discussed. If you pay these taxes through an escrow account, your lender may send you a form with the amount you paid in the previous year. Money deposited into your escrow account does not qualify for a tax deduction. You can only deduct actual taxes paid out of the account during the current tax year.

On the other hand, if you pay your property taxes directly to the municipality, use your records to determine this amount. In the year you purchased the house, you probably reimbursed the seller for prepaid real estate taxes. If this is the case, you can deduct this amount with your real estate taxes as well.

Tax credits are more valuable on your return because they reduce your tax bill dollar-for-dollar. With energy-saving improvements in your home, you can earn energy credits. You earn a credit for up to 10% of the cost of qualifying energy-efficient skylights, roofs, outside doors and windows, insulation systems, water boilers, central air conditioners, furnaces, water heaters, and heat pumps. Additional credits are available for advanced energy-efficiency equipment such as solar-powered water heaters and generators.

If you decide to lease your property, you will need to record rental income on your return. However, as a renter, there are more deductions available to you. Any repairs on the rental property are fully deductible, given the repairs are ordinary, necessary and reasonable. For example, if the air conditioning is broken or the faucet is leaking, those are ordinary and necessary. Also, repainting after a tenant moves out.

Another deduction is travel. Anywhere that you must travel in order to perform business as it relates to your rental property, you can deduct. It is important to have good records on your mileage. Track all the miles spent on the business and keep an odometer count from January 1 and December 31 of the tax year.

There are two methods to deducting mileage on your return; you can track the actual miles traveled for your rental property and multiply by the standard mileage rate noted by the IRS, or you can calculate the actual expense of maintaining your properties. This would involve tracking repairs on your business vehicle, maintenance, gasoline, and payments. You will also have to calculate the percentage of the vehicle that is used for your rental properties. Only that percentage of actual expenses is deductible. For example, if you make a $200 monthly payment, spend $3000 in gas and $600 on maintenance and repairs, then in one year, you have spent $6,000 on your vehicle. If in one year, you drive 20,000 miles, but only 5,000 miles are for your rental property, then you can only claim $1,500, or 25 percent, of your actual car expenses.

In addition to mileage, you can deduct long distance travel if you're using it to travel overnight to your rental property. When traveling for your property, you can deduct airfare, hotel bills, meals and other necessary expenses incurred while you are away. Keep clear records that indicate why you traveled and what business was handled while you were away.

Do you work from home to handle the administrative work of real estate rentals? If yes, then you can deduct the space devoted to office work. There are two methods for calculating the deduction on home offices. In order to qualify for the home office deduction, you must use the space regularly, exclusively and out of necessity. For either method, you will need to know the square footage of the space you use to conduct business. Home offices could be as large as a room or as small as a desk. Get out your measuring tape and figure out how much space is used and calculate which home office calculation method will yield you the biggest deduction.

Similar to the travel deduction, the regular method for calculating your home office tax deduction requires you to keep records of all expenses for the home. These expenses may include mortgage interest, insurance, utilities, repairs, and depreciation. After calculating your total expenses, you then calculate the percentage of those expenses that is related to maintaining your rental properties and deduct that amount. The new simplified method is a standard deduction of $5 per square foot of home used for business with a maximum of 300 square feet. Depreciation is not an allowable deduction when using the simplified option. Take the time to do comparisons to see which calculation method has the higher deduction for you. Although the standard method takes more time, it could help you save big on your return.

If you hire someone to manage your properties or perform services, you can deduct wages as a business expense. As a property owner, you can hire employees and independent contractors. Wages for both are deductible. The differentiation between the two is that as an employer, you must withhold federal and state taxes and pay half of the worker's Social Security and Medicare taxes for employees. You do not have any state or federal payroll tax obligations for independent contractors. Independent contractors include plumbers, carpenters, painters, roofers, gardeners, and anyone else performing a service on your property. Another deduction is for legal and professional services. Monies paid to attorneys, accountants, real estate investment advisors and other professionals that are necessary for day-to-day administrative work and overall business planning are deductible as long as the services you receive are related to your rental properties.

Lastly, in the event of a casualty, you are able to claim a deduction. A casualty is damage, destruction or loss of property as a result of sudden, unexpected or unusual events. Allowable events to qualify for the deduction include, but are not limited to fires, floods, vandalism, and storms. Any damage to the property that is not abnormal, such as a roof collapsing due to years of deterioration or normal winds blowing a branch through your window is not deductible as a casualty loss. Your deduction amount will depend on if the property experienced total or partial loss. For partial loss, you must subtract any insurance you receive or are expecting, and calculate the decrease in the property's fair marker or the adjusted basis of the property. Adjusted basis is the original cost of the property plus any improvements minus any deductions. The lesser of the two calculations is deductible. For a total loss, your deduction is calculated as salvage value subtracted from adjusted basis. Salvage value is the value of any remains from the damage. You will also have to reduce that calculation by any insurance monies collected. Your final total is your deductible loss.

Note that if you receive any additional payments or settlements, such as repairs or payments from a tenant, federal disaster loan forgiveness, or a court award for a settlement, then you must subtract these from your claimed loss. The IRS is not looking to pay you twice, but rather allow you to claim actual loss.

You can borrow home equity loans if you've built your equity up enough, to finance anything. A home equity loan is a type of second mortgage and is offered either as a standard fix-rate or a line of credit. Terms usually range from five to 15 years and homeowners will go through a process similar to the one they used to purchase their home in the beginning. Interest on these loans are deductible up to $100,000. Home equity loans can be advantageous.

If the down payment on your home is less than 20% of the home's cost, the buyer will likely pay a premium for mortgage insurance, an extra fee that protects the lender if the loan isn't repaid. For mortgages issued after 2007, home buyers can deduct premiums.

Insurance

Purchasing title insurance is recommended, as it protects the homebuyer and mortgage lender from any title claims. Title is the owner's right to possess and use the property. Title claims include deeds, bankruptcy proceedings, judgment liens, tax liens, liens for repairs or improvements to the property, and probate proceedings. If a seller does not have the right to transfer full ownership of the property to you, title insurance will cover you. Coverage for title insurance is not typically expensive, and could potentially protect you from losing the house. At the time of closing, there are sometimes unforeseen issues, such as building permit violations or forgeries. In these cases, title insurance will benefit you.

Typically, title insurance includes a lender's policy and a borrower's policy. The lender's policy should state that legal defense costs and any mortgage payments that can't be made because of loss of property will be covered and reimbursed. A borrower's policy will cover the homebuyer's legal fees and other losses. Before issuing an insurance policy, title companies will perform a title search and look through public records for the house including wills, trusts, tax records and bankruptcy filings. This is advantageous because the title report will provide the potential buyer with history and areas for cause. If something serious is found, the potential buyer can call off the sale.

If you choose not to get title insurance, you are opening yourself up to potential claims that didn't come up in the title search. A house is one of the biggest investments you will ever make. Title insurance can help provide peace of mind if any major issues regarding ownership ever arise.

Business Plan and Budgeting

Budgeting and finances are essential to developing a business plan. Before taking a dive into real estate investing, you need to take a step back and define your purpose, practices and sales goals. Your business plan should be comprehensive enough that you have clearly defined goals and know what strategies and tactics you will use in order to meet those goals. Along with finances, your business plan should state how much you expect to earn over a period of time, what your budget is, how much of your sales or rental incomes will cover expenses and more. Your business plan should use SMART goals (specific, measurable, achievable, realistic and time-bound). The length of your business plan will vary. You may want to develop a plan just for your first year, or you may want to project out for the next three to five years – the choice is yours.

Most business plans include a mission statement. Why are you entering into the real estate investment business? What do you want to be known for? What services and benefits do you offer? The answers to these questions will provide you with a mission statement. While real estate is what you do, who you are is just as important. The mission statement of your business plan is an extension of your properties and tells more about who you are in the market.

Next, set your goals. By investing in real estate, what do you plan to achieve? Be specific in setting your goals. Set small goals that are achievable. You can also use milestones to ensure that you are progressing towards an end goal. You also want a timeframe that is reasonable in achieving your goals. Goals do not have to be financial, but should be measurable. An example of this is setting a goal of spending at least 10 hours a week researching properties and putting in bids.

Your strategy for real estate investing will be your strategy. There are many ways to make money in real estate, but you want to pick the one that best fits with your lifestyle, fits within your budget, and you find enjoyable. The last thing you want is to make lots of money and not be able to enjoy it because of all the grunt work you feel you're doing. By only picking one strategy, you can build your reputation with a niche audience. After reading through this guide, you will have a deeper understanding of the different investment strategies. These include flipping houses, single-family and multi-family properties, vacation homes and more. These strategies will be discussed later in this book.

Who is your audience? Define your market niche, as this will be the basis for your decision on what strategies and tactics to use to grow your business. Your audience will be determined by who your properties are most suited for. Perhaps you are looking to help low-income individuals and families find affordable housing. Your strategy for doing this could be finding less expensive real estate, fixing it up and making a small profit from multiple families. Think about the strategy that you will use to begin investing and figure out who will best benefit from your service.

You will also want to do research on the market. In the example of low-income individuals, you will want to know what the demand is. Are you able to secure any additional financing because that is your niche audience? How many other realtors are also targeting that population? What makes you unique? What percentage of sales in your market included that market niche? These questions will force you to think critically about your investment and your ability to succeed. You also want to ensure that there is enough market to go around. Defining your niche can either help you stand out among competitors or it can make you blend in. That's where research becomes key. Location may also be included in your market niche. Do you want to focus on particular neighborhoods in your community? Are you willing to take any property that's available? Either way, you will want to define that here.

Now, here's the fun part – the numbers. After going through the previous steps to developing your business plan, you should now have the who, what, when, where and why you're doing this. While your strategies tell you how you will reach a goal, you need the numbers to back it up. Include a financial statement that describes your current financial standing as it relates to real estate investing. You will want to look at what equity and assets are you willing and able to invest. You could also be in the position where you do not have anything to start with. That's okay, but be sure to write that down. This will be the most fluid part of your business plan as your financial standing is always changing.

Along with your business plan, you could keep quarterly and annual financial statements that keep track of your income, expenses, assets and liabilities. This will help you keep a close eye on cash flow and net worth and should be assessed against your goals as another way of making sure you're making steps to achieve them. How much money do you need to make in your first year? Second year? Third year? And so on if your business plan is longer than three years. Research basic figures and trends to determine this amount. Basic figures would include average sale price for properties. You will also have expenses. Expenses will include payments, broker fees, car and technology fees, and marketing and advertising. Think through all the expenses you have and for how long you will have them. Are your expenses one-time or recurring?

While documenting income and expenses is important, be strategic in thinking about how you will generate income from real estate investing. Think beyond your first sale. How will you turn a profit on every purchase? If your strategy doesn't work, then what's plan B?

In order to meet goals, you will need to conduct a certain number of transactions. You will not get a sale from every meeting you have; therefore, you need to generate a list of leads. Calculate in the financials of your business plan how many transactions and leads you need in order to meet your goals.

Once you have established your current financial standing, set your criteria. You will be eager to find deals, but you need to define what an acceptable deal is to you. If you are investing in a rental property, what are your cash flow requirements? If you plan on flipping houses, what is the most amount of time you will spend fixing up the house? If you want to buy and hold property, in what conditions will you certainly not sell? Think about deals from all angles. You will want to consider deals you are making, as well as deals being brought to you. This section of your business plan is to protect you from becoming emotionally attached to a deal. Perhaps you really like a family that is interested in renting your unit, but they don't check all the boxes for your rental criteria. You can walk away from the deal with peace of mind because you stuck to your criteria.

With that being said, consider having a flexibility statement in your business plan. You do not want a statement that is too broad that you are constantly wavering from your criteria, but you want something that isn't to narrow that you feel constrained to your business plan. Find the sweet spot. A good rule of thumb is for your flexibility statement to be based on the current market trends.

In order to reach your goals, you need to take action. But how can you act if no one knows who you are? Marketing is how you will spread the word on properties you're selling or looking to purchase. Your marketing section of the business plan should explain how you will motivate others to work with you.

Basic marketing strategy setting includes looking at the marketing mix, which are the four P's that drive individuals to a business: price, product, place, and promotion. Each of these four P's provide you with a target market. Use this knowledge to drive where you allocate your marketing dollars. The four P's are also a way to delve deeper into goal setting. You want your goals to be specific, so an example would be "In order to close on three single-family homes in the next 18 months, I need to generate 100 leads in my first year. I will generate leads through my website and purchase paid advertising on Google that targets married couples, ages 35 to 50, in the Portland, Oregon area making more than $100,000 a year for buying single-family units." Action steps to achieving these goals could include taking a course on Google advertising or refreshing the advertising language every three weeks.

Marketing may require another set of hands if that is not your strong suit. In the next section of your business plan, you will determine what the key roles of your team are and how they will help you implement your plan. This includes potential employees or contractors that are essential to day-to-day operations or individuals that you will work with on a regular basis, like a printing vendor, tax professional or lawyer. Define the function each role provides and any responsibilities the person may be held accountable for. Other key team members include mortgage brokers, professional contractors, realtors, property managers, escrow officers and insurance agents. These team members may not be employed by you, but they are essential to helping you meet your goals.

So, you have now put all of this in place into your business plan. You're almost to the end! Your last consideration is exit strategies and backup plans. While there are backup plans throughout the entirety of your business plan, in this section, you will define your end game. You purchased a piece of property or multiple properties, now how will you rid yourself of it. Strategies include leasing, and selling with a real estate agent, seller financing or on your own. Similar to the flexibility statement, include backup strategies for exiting a deal.

With that, you're done! Depending on where you are in your business, you can decide to put plans for incorporating your business. When you're first getting started, you may not think about it, but in the long term and as you plan on exchanging larger amounts of money, you should incorporate your business. Incorporation protects you as an individual. In the event that something happens, and an entity goes after you, if you are not incorporated, then someone could go after your personal assets. It is best to keep the two separate, but consult with a real estate attorney to help you make this important decision, as incorporation comes with a new set of tax liabilities and fees.

I strongly encourage you to invest the time necessary for preparing for a better future. Ask yourself the hard questions. Set SMART goals. Stay on track and measure your success. Be careful and thoughtful in tracking your financials. You should look at your financials on an ongoing basis and reassess your plan every year. The real estate market changes often enough that you should require it of yourself to ensure your goals line up with what's realistic given the market. Your business plan will be a step in the right direction for establishing a sustainable real estate investment career.

Chapter 3 – Inspecting Houses

When you go out to purchase investment properties, do you know what you are looking for? By creating a simple criteria checklist, you can help narrow down your selection and focus on properties that you feel comfortable buying, owning and selling. Investment property criteria includes town, neighborhood, square footage, lot size, property conditions, number of units, cap rate, appreciation potential, and cash flow potential. You may have additional criteria that you're looking for, or some of the items listed above are not important to you. You need to develop your own checklist that is aligned with what you are looking for. This will save you time and be more manageable, as you can't visit every available property.

Due diligence is a step taken by a person or business before making an investment. A house inspection is a large part of a home buyer's due diligence. When you inspect houses, be aware that in the area where houses are located, there may be a lot of houses for sale. If this is the case, look at the competition. See what homes are selling and for what price. You will also want to get an accurate after repair value (ARV) from a real estate broker. Getting friendly with a real estate agent will help you because if they think that you will give them your business, they will be happy to provide you with information.

There are several things that you need to take into account when you inspect a home. These are as follows:

- How the house compares with others on the market in the same area

- How the price compares with other houses

- What the home offers

- What disadvantages there are

Before deciding to invest, you should also take a look at the neighborhood, school districts, and general location. These elements will affect investment, so it is important for you to have a clear understanding of your potential to sell or lease. Other considerations include nearby shopping, transportation (where's the nearest highway or public transportation line?), and health facilities.

Let me go into this in more detail because at the moment, you may not be accustomed to the housing market. If this is your first investment, you need to get it right. The first of the criteria about is pretty obvious because taking a look at other homes within the area will give you an idea of what the market is like. If you are looking at a family home, is the area in which the home is located suitable for family life? You need to know what's available and at what price and whether the home can fill some gap in the market.

Family homes need:

- Access to good schools
- Safe streets for kids to play
- Good transport links
- Good shopping facilities

Executive accommodation would need other things:

- Up to date and modern accommodation
- Nearness to transport links
- Parking
- Availability of evening entertainment in the area

Different kinds of people need different things. Knowing the market that you're going into is important. If you market is saturated with family homes, the executive bachelor pad may not be the best option and you may end up losing money on the transaction.

What disadvantages are there?

The moment you enter a home, you should be looking for problems. Are the floors solid or are there areas that squeak? Are there repairs that were never finished? What is the decor? Does the kitchen and bathroom need replacing? Are the floors in the property in good condition? What state is the woodwork in? Is there double glazing and if so to what standard? Is there off street parking? How much work will need to be done before the house can be put onto the market and what will the repairs cost you? Very importantly, what is the condition of the roof?

You are better off going into a home with your eyes open to all of the detail. If you notice old electrical sockets hanging off the wall, chances are you may need to rewire the house. If the tile is cracked, why? If this is on an upstairs floor, you may have to replace the tile, but it's quite likely that the subfloor that it is sitting on is the reason for the cracks. You need to be a detective to a certain degree.

Take a note pad or clipboard and note everything that you see. Take a camera points and shoot images of anything you are in doubt about so that you can discuss this with contractors as needed.

When you have inspected, if you are serious about making a purchase, never part with your money before you have assessed things correctly and do get a property appraisal that highlights any of the things that you may have missed. These are done by professionals who know what to look for.

Property appraisals estimate the property's value based on factors such as structural condition, location, amenities, and recent sales of nearby properties. Appraisals usually take less than a day. Within days, an appraisal report is sent to the mortgage lender. With some real estate offers, you may receive an appraisal contingency. Contingencies allow you to get out of a deal without losing any money. Appraisal contingencies can either say if you are unable to have the property appraised at or above the value of the purchase price, then you can back out; or if you are unable to have the property appraised at or above the value of the purchase price, then you can ask the seller to drop the price, and if refused, you can back out.

Chapter 4 – Getting Ready to Make an Offer

Before making an offer, you need to understand the market. While you can't predict what will happen in the market, it does change slowly. When investing, it is good to know the difference between a buyer's market and a seller's market. A buyer's market is when there is more supply than demand. While there are people out looking to sell houses, but no one snatching it up, that's when you swoop in. In a buyer's market, sellers may have to accept a lower price if they want to sell their home at all. This is when buyers can get a great deal. In a seller's market, the demand is greater than supply. As the economy improves, more people can spend money on real estate. This creates more competition in the market for properties, which is ideal for the seller. There are several things that will tell you how desperate someone is to sell a home. Signs that there is room for negotiation in the price are the following:

- The house has been on the market a long time

- The house is priced too highly compared with other houses in the area

- There are repairs to be done that will be costly

- The owners have already moved out so are desperate to break links with their past life

- The home has been neglected

These are all circumstantial items but they give you a clue about the property and they also tell you whether the home is likely to sell at its existing price. The real estate agent will be able to tell you if the price has been dropped recently. They will also be able to talk to you about the circumstances of the seller. Be friendly. Learn as much as you can because all of this information can help you to get a bargain.

When you have your property report, you will be able to make a more detailed assessment of what it will cost to do any renovations that may be needed, although that may not stop you from making an offer. If there is a lot of interest in the home, you may be able to make a tentative offer, bearing in mind the repairs that you have already noted with a provision that the offer is subject to a satisfactory property report. That covers you in case there is something drastic that you didn't pick up on when you were looking around the house.

If you are dealing with buying the house through a real estate agent, you should never make the offer direct with the seller. Talk things through reasonably with the real estate agent. For example:

"Taking into account the amount of repairs needed to get the house up to date, I would like to propose an offer of $ X amount subject to a satisfactory property report."

The real estate agent will have been working with the seller and should have a good idea of whether your offer comes anywhere near the amount that the seller needs. In fact, you get more information from real estate agents because selling the house is their main priority. However, don't be talked into something that your instinct tells you is a higher price than you are prepared to pay because you will inevitably stand to lose more. The normal procedure is for the real estate agent to contact the seller and to come back to you either with a counter offer, which you can walk away from or details of what the seller is likely to accept.

When you are making offers on houses, you may find that you are left with this sense of anticipation. Do not telephone again. It shows the real estate agent that you are too keen and that's not a good thing. If you show all of your cards, you leave yourself vulnerable and it's not worth it. There will always be another house and another possibility. Do not be talked into paying more for the home than you feel it is worth, bearing in mind the checks you have done against other houses and also the amount of repairs you would have to do to get the house up to the same condition as houses that are selling for more money. The more you give away at this stage, the less chance you have of turning a profit.

When you are looking for a house to live in rather than to flip, you should still look from a commercial viewpoint. This is probably the biggest investment you will make in your life. At a later stage in life, you may want to sell it on. If it takes you an absolute fortune to get it into shape, you may not get your money back on it and it's not worth getting yourself into that situation in the first place. If you have doubts about the costs and are being pushed to make a higher offer, walk away.

Be sure of what you are getting into and don't sign anything until you have all of the facts and are happy with them. In real estate, profit comes from the difference between the initial cost of the property and what it sells for in the end. Always keep that top of mind.

Chapter 5 – Refurbishment

A scope of work is a detailed list of everything that needs to be completed in order to resell the home. Your property inspection will be a big part of your scope of work as you will want to fix any problems that came up during that process. When you know that you are going to buy a property to flip, you also have to know the timescale for the work that needs to be done. If you are completely new to the process when it comes to the property, you need to get all of your job bids in from electricians, plumbers, drywall experts, and whoever else will be doing to work to get the house into the best condition possible. There is a set order to work and if this is not respected, you will find it costs you more to actually get things done.

Initial preparation – If you have plans about what you are going to do to the house, you will know if internal walls need knocking down or if you need a kitchen ripped out or a bathroom ripped out. The initial preparation stages are done by someone who is a laborer and these people usually charge you a day rate. It is my experience that you need to be as hands on as possible to save you money. Remember, if you leave someone who is on a day rate to their own devices, they may stretch the job out simply to earn more. If you are there during this time, you can make sure that this doesn't happen.

This initial preparation needs doing before you have qualified contractor into the property because it's basically getting all the bad stuff out. You may be able to save money in some areas. For example, the kitchen units may be good quality and have a lot of life left in them, but you may want to replace the doors of the units. At this initial stage, you need to have ongoing notes so that you can order all of the items that you need so that they are there when your qualified workmen need them. It costs you money to have contractors waiting for building materials to be delivered.

First fix – This is the stage that happens before dry wall is done. This includes things like fixing subfloor problems, assessing the damage you may have found while ripping things out etc. You may have found rot and perhaps there is asbestos that needs to be removed from the property. You can't do this work. You will need to make sure that a qualified person comes in and does it. Pipework and wiring that goes behind walls is done at this stage. You will need to schedule plumbers, electricians and other contractors to come in stages so they will not be vying for the same spaces at the same time. This time will also include being aware of what lighting needs to be installed to bring the house up to modern standards as all the wires need to be laid ready for this.

Second fix – This includes all of the items such as dry wall additions, tiling and the things that you will see such as kitchen worktops, fitting kitchen units, making sure that all the sockets are put in place. Make sure that you know when tilers are going to do their work because this needs to be done in conjunction with the kitchen or bathroom fitting and is important. Similarly, you don't want to do floors when you know there is still messy work to be done unless you are able to protect them fully.

To keep this organized, make sure that you use a spreadsheet. Even if you don't know how to use a professional one from your computer, at least create a listing that shows all of the dates and all of the times that you need workmen to be at the house so that you can schedule everything and it runs smoothly. A potential mistake you can make here is having contractors on site before they are required. This costs YOU extra money because even if they are sitting around doing nothing, YOU are getting charged for them being there. You may see this as unreasonable. However, if you scheduled them in to start a job and they are there but the building materials are not you are still responsible for their time.

Ordering of all the materials that you need for the house must be done in advance. Try to work with off the shelf items as much as you can because anything that is made to measure will cost you extra and may take more time to be delivered and this can cost you extra money.

Make sure that your contractor's quotes are all inclusive and that they are itemized so that you can drop items off the list if necessary to keep your budget in trim. Do not change your mind and add extra items. It is far better to make a thorough plan for your refurbishment rather than add things at a stage that will cost you extra money.

Setting and sticking to a schedule is essential when flipping houses. The quicker you move, the higher your profit. Remember, as long as you own a property, you must make payments. When looking at your budget and timeline, look at what renovations need to be done to the home. For projects that are not time-intensive, such as painting, appliance upgrades and landscaping, you can turn the house around in weeks. However, if major electrical or plumbing work needs to be done or the roof and siding need repair, it could take months to complete your project. The length of time of the house flip does affect your bottom line, so be sure to make estimations ahead of time, which will help you determine if you are making a worthy investment. Keep an eye on your progress so that at any given time you know where you are on the project. Develop a timeline for getting your work done. You should make a detailed list of renovations and when they will be done. Share this with your team, as one contractor may need to be finished before the next can come in. Take on your largest projects first.

Unfortunately, everything isn't always in our control. The day you schedule the painters may be the same day as a major rainstorm. By scheduling the big work first, it will help your schedule. Repairing the roof will set you back further than rescheduling a paint job. Major fixes include rewiring the house; fixing broken bathtubs, showers, and sinks; and patching up walls, ceilings, and door holes. Work from the outside in. You want the exterior of the home to look sellable as soon as possible. After that work is done, you can place your for sale sign outside to begin generating leads for the property.

Make sure also that your contractors are available on the dates that you need them to be and that they have been tied down to a finishing date because this gives them the incentive to get the job done and leaves you knowing what stage the renovation is going to be at, at all times during the renovation of the house.

Flipping houses requires paperwork and obtaining permits. Do your research ahead of time to know what permits are necessary for completing the project. You can apply for them before you begin working. Failing to file for a permit can cause a work stoppage, which puts your project timeline at risk and will cost you money. With contractors on your property, you will also need insurance coverage for the property itself and the workers. Keep documentation of your coverage, along with receipts and contracts. There may be problems that you do not expect. By keeping your paperwork straight, you will be better equipped for handling any issues.

Chapter 6 – Work You Can do Yourself

There may be ways to save money during the renovation of a house and if you are trying to stick within a budget, it's a good idea to try the following ideas to help to save you money. If you have skills that you can employ you can save a fortune. Shortly we'll discuss some of the ways that you can try and save money.

In addition to saving money, there are improvements that will increase the value of the home. Kitchens and bathrooms increase the prices of homes. Sleek and updated appliances and fixtures are popular with buyers, so by adding these to the home, you are able to drive up the selling price. Do your research to determine if the cost of the upgrades is greater than the value it will add to the home. If it is, you may want to forego kitchen and bathroom upgrades. Adding a deck also raises the value of a home. Minor landscaping can also boost value.

Laboring – During the initial ripping out of the old fixtures and fittings, it doesn't take a lot of skill, but it does take many hands! If you are there and able to supervise, you can also help with some of the jobs such as ripping out old kitchen and bathroom fittings. Laboring isn't that hard. It's just a case of getting involved in the day to day processes that are going on at the house. This helps you to keep your costs down. For example, ripping out old tiling or taking out an old bathroom are not that hard, but need doing. If you can free yourself up to help with this, you will be saving money. You can also repaint, change fittings, repave entrances or add new handles. If you feel certain you can't do this work on your own, find cheaper labor like high school or college students to help.

Help with contractors – When you approach contractors for their quotes, do ask if there is anything that you can do to help out and to make the costs a little less. There may also be labor that they are happy for you to pitch in on and this can save money. For example, in one renovation, I was asked to tear out the walls to get them ready to take additional wiring and once I was shown how this was done was able to save the electrician a lot of time. He also plastered after he put in sockets and if he had made any holes in the walls. If you think that you are up to it, you can probably do this just as well as he can and save yourself money.

Just be honest and upfront about your budget and try to win over the favor of your contractors. Areas that you can help with may be all the decoration that needs doing at the end of the job. If you feel that you are up to the task, then it will be worthwhile doing it. If, however, this is not something you are good at, then make sure that you can help by doing clearing up and preparation to save money. Don't get in the way of the contractors but show that you are willing to get your hands dirty if it helps you to keep your work within the budget that you have set.

When you start to clear out your first house, you will find that there are always things that you can do to save money. Remember though, at this point, you have defined your target audience so make a plan that appeals to your audience, not you. You can be on site while the work is being performed and will be able to make sure that you are getting things done correctly and in a timely manner. When all the contractors have finished their work, the actual preparation and finishing touches are what make that house sell. People want to see neutral interiors, so don't make the house too colorful. They want to be able to imagine their lives within that home. If that means that you can use any of the existing fittings within a house, it's cheaper for you to actually hire a sanding machine than to replace flooring. It's cheaper to take off cupboard doors and replace them yourself than to install a new kitchen.

The contractors where you really cannot skimp are electricians, plumbers, carpenters, and roofers. However, having a first class carpenter available, you may be able to cut corners using their expertise. They may also be willing to work with you and welcome your interaction with them during the course of the work.

At the end of the day, it's your investment. You are the client, but you should never get so blasé about the work that you think yourself above doing any of the physical labor yourself. If you get into this state, and I have known people who have, you will spend more for your work than had you rolled up your sleeves and done the work yourself. Time costs money.

For those who are willing to pitch in on the work, there are multiple ways that you can save. You can also make yourself available to help out when you see that contractors need you, but remember to ask in advance. Some contractors work faster when they are left to it, so getting to know the character of your contractors is essential. Be welcoming, provide them with something to drink as they work and try to create a relationship that works well for both you and them.

Chapter 7 – Marketing

Before you are able to put a house on the market, you need to be sure that the market is ripe and ready for it. You should have done a lot of investigation of the housing market in the area where your house is BEFORE you bought it, but as soon as the house is ready for inspection, you need to know how the current market is doing. Check your newspapers to see the prices of houses in the area. Make sure that the presentation of the home is first rate. People can be put off by arriving at a house to see garbage outside. They want to see a pretty front yard. Make sure the windows are clean and that the house is presented in a neutral fashion.

As you are showing the home, consider staging. Staging is where you make the home look as though someone lives there by placing art, and other décor around the home. You may want to consider renting furniture to put into the home. You can visit discount stores for furniture and décor, or include money for a rental company to come in and stage the home. Staging is a strategy used by real estate agents, as staged homes tend to sell quicker. Often people are more tempted by seeing a home with living spaces already set up so they can start to visualize their own use of the space. Think about when you shop for a place to live. Rooms with furniture are easier to imagine yourself living in, versus when there isn't furniture.

The idea is that you present the house as a potential blank canvas, but with enough in it for people to be able to consider it as a potential home. If it's cold and doesn't look that nice, they may not be able to see past this, so you do need to dress the home ready for viewings.

You need to aim at the particular market you think the house suits. When the real estate agent calls, make sure that they have the right details to share with potential buyers. Marketing the house is essential and you need to be satisfied with the photographs. If you are not, take better ones and ask them to adjust their documentation. They will usually be okay with this if you approach it in a pleasant way.

Choosing the right real estate agent is essential. You need to know that the real estate agent has a good clientele base, a good quality website, plenty of contacts, and the potential to advertise your property sufficiently. If you find that one local real estate agency is more prominent than another, then this may be a time to make a choice between the two.

You also need to know if you are permitted to advertise yourself. When people go into flipping houses, often they create a website to give their properties more prominence although in the initial stages your energy would be better spent on a real estate agent. There may be general real estate websites where you can advertise but it's helpful to work with with a real estate agency and ask them if you can point inquiries toward them. Find out if there are discounts for sole agency. That means that you leave the property with one agent and they charge you less. Find out as well if they are willing to give a discount if a potential purchaser gets near to the asking price.

The price at which you market the property should be competitive, but it should also be high enough to make sure that if someone makes an offer, they feel like they are getting a bargain. Add 10% to what you'd like to get for the home and hope that someone will really come up with the price that you want. Make sure that the house is warm and welcoming at all times. Presentation is everything. Also make sure you ask for feedback so you can make adjustments if something has been spotted that you didn't think about.

Turning a profit on a house should be possible if you have studied the market before you started the renovation of the house and know what kind of accommodation people want. The house that you bought may have had many rooms, but by turning it into open plan, you may also bring more people in to look at the house. The marketing of the home is vital. You may even want to have an open house day, but if you do this, make sure that the house is perfect on those days, so that people don't just turn around and drive away.

The more welcoming you can be the better. Walk through the house and look for strong points to give ideas to the real estate agent about things you feel will sell the place. Make sure all jobs are done and that the potential purchasers have nothing in the way of repairs that need doing to use as bargaining power when they make offers.

There are various sales ploys that you can use, like providing visitors with freshly brewed coffee which always smells inviting and makes a home feel great. You may even want to offer visitors a buffet snack, but that's up to you and the real estate agent. If you are having an open day, make sure you maximize the potential by lining up the advertising so that people have time to make arrangements to be there. Ask your real estate agent what times of day give the best results. If you are aiming at families, then there may be times when parents are more available to come and look at the house and even if this means marketing the house at a weekend.

We are living in a digital age. So many people are now getting their information and making initial decisions on large purchases based on what they see online. You can be more competitive by marketing through online advertising. While traditional marketing methods will still get you results, the internet will provide you with customizable tools and analytic data that can help you determine if your advertising is effective, or more importantly, who your audience is. You may think you already know that, but by monitoring who is watching your online activity, you can be surprised and learn new things about the market.

Two of the top marketing tools are Facebook and Google. Facebooks allows you to target ads based on Facebook users' interests, demographics, location, and Facebook connections. For example, if you happened to have a medieval castle property, you could target potential buyers in the area who have an interest in medieval times and are connected to groups that share content on medieval properties. Google allows you to target your ads based on users' searches, web history, and location. In the same example, you could target individuals who recently googled medieval property in your area.

When targeting ads, the fewer people you reach, the more targeted your ad is and the more likely the individuals who are reached will engage with your content. You want the money you're paying for advertising to have a high return on investment, meaning each ad should yield X amount of leads and X amount of transactions. The payment structure for online advertising makes it easy to track conversions. Pay-per-click advertising means you only pay when someone clicks on an ad and goes to your site. With clear messaging that is targeted towards individuals with interests and demographics in your area, you will attract the right people to potentially buy your property.

Pay-per-click advertising is based on a bid. The more you are willing to invest, the more likely your target market will see your ads. While setting up your ad, you will be prompted to enter the amount per click you want to pay. If your bid is too low, you will be outbid and your ad will not be shown to your audience. If your ad isn't shown, you aren't losing any money, but you also aren't gaining any leads. You can choose between setting a daily budget or a monthly budget. This means if you set a daily budget of $15, your ad will run throughout the day until you max out on your budget.

Once you find the bid that will get you noticed, you want your ad to be eye-catching and entice your audience to actually click and convert. You will want a photo that grabs a potential buyer in. Create a title that will stand out. Consider asking a question. Your description should be factual and emotional. Appeal directly to your audience by using language they can connect with. For example, to appeal to first-time homebuyers, you may use a photo of someone getting the keys to their house or signing the papers with a smile. The ad title could be "Are you ready to own a home of your own?" with a description that includes features of the home and what a future in the home could look like.

Your ad will connect to another webpage. You will want to capture leads on the landing page or your website. Be sure to have a form that visitors can fill out with their phone number and email address. The shorter your form is, the more likely a visitor will fill it out. If you do not yet have a website, you can design one using pre-made templates on a number of design and host websites, or you could hire a freelancer to set it up for you.

Websites are great for capturing leads from online advertising. With any advertisement, you want there to be a clear call-to-action. However, a website can be a living page with information about your listings. By building an online reputation, you could drive regular traffic to your website. Your reputation can be built through commenting on other real estate blogs or websites, engaging with real estate influencers online, writing your own blog with content that is relevant to both buyers and sellers, and attending webinars or online chat sessions and being an active participant.

Reputation breeds organic reach while paid advertising is paid reach. The more organic reach you have, the fewer dollars you need to put towards advertising your properties. People in your area may already know you're trustworthy and want to work with you. But again, this takes time and patience to build.

Chapter 8 – The Potential of Buying a House at Auction

If you are thinking of buying a house at auction, you need to know what you are getting yourself into. People want quick sales, but there may be reasons behind it other than the obvious. You need to investigate the house thoroughly but you only have a short space of time in which to do it. To make the most of this situation, you need to follow a set procedure:

Find an auction

Do you have a list of auctioneers in your area? Call their office periodically to find out when they have upcoming auctions. You can also check listings on the web and in your local newspaper. Pay attention to your streets. If a house will be auctioned, there are usually signs out front announcing the date and phone number.

Attending auctions, even if you don't plan on bidding, is a great way of learning about the different auctioneers' selling practices and how they call for bids. There may also be auctioneer fees that the winning bidder must pay in addition to the final price. Read the terms and conditions of the auction to see if you notice patterns.

Set up your financing

Know from your bank how much you can borrow at short notice and work out your budget the same way you would for buying on a regular sale. The house is only worth a set price which should consist of:

- The asking price
- The cost of refurbishment
- The potential asking price

If the house costs $200,000 and the potential repairs look like they could come to $90,000, you will need to have $290,000 available to you, but you will also need some kind of assurance that the fully refurbished house could see at more than $290,000 to make a profit.

Because of that you will also need to be aware of the real estate market in the area where the house is located. Look at similar properties. Ask around. Be aware of what you are getting yourself into because you don't have time to go back on your word that you will buy the property. You need to know what the house is worth to you.

Inspecting the property

We have already told you in another chapter what to look for when you are buying a property but bear in mind that when you are buying at auction, you have a limited time to get all your estimates together. If you can take your contractor with you, you may have to pay them a little to give you the time but it will be worth it because they will know what to look out for and will be able to give you an idea on remedial costings. You can contact an attorney, or do a search on your own for information regarding the title of the property.

If there are questions that you have about the property, make sure that you have asked them before the sales day. They will be dealing with a lot of inquiries and it's up to you to ask relevant questions. You don't have the same level of control when you buy at auction so if this means writing things down, do so and make sure that you know exactly what it is that you are buying. Reputable auctioneers or property owners will disclose information on property liens and outstanding taxes that may exist to all potential home buyers before accepting bids.

Whether you plan on living in the property, renting it or flipping it, visit the town hall that governs the property you want to buy. Find out more information on by-laws, zoning issues, ordinances, toxic or hazardous waste issues, and anything else that may affect your purchasing decision. Zoning may affect your ability to flip, and by-laws may affect your ability to rent. An initial conversation with a town hall representative will help you determine if the property being auctioned aligns with your business plan.

Decide on a set budget

This is vital because it is very easy to get carried away with bidding. If the home reaches the amount that you have decided is viable and there are still bids coming, walk away. You won't make money on the house and it's one of the biggest mistakes that real estate flippers make. They hear others bidding and they up their bidding beyond what is reasonable. Then when it comes to renovating the house, they are already working with a shortfall of money, making the budget very tight and may end up taking a loss on the property.

On the auction day

Have a set budget for how much you can spend on the house and do not go beyond it. When the auction is in progress, don't be too keen to get your bids in. Wait and see how the bidding goes so that you know who your competition is. Go in with a bid when you are ready and remember that you have a top budget and stick to it.

If you are the winner of the auction, you will be expected to pay for the property up front. It will be worthwhile finding out what fees are involved when you purchase the house and just before the auction, you can find this out from asking the staff at the auction house. This kind of purchase is suitable for those who are cash buyers because they know their exact financial situation and also know how much money they have left to do the repairs. If you do not have cash, but have arranged a loan, you have to work out your potential profit less whatever that loan will cost you and you should make sure that the lender is prepared for early repayment and will not charge you too much in the way of fees for early repayment.

Chapter 9 – Flipping Houses in General

Flipped homes are typically bought and sold within six months. Flipping a house is when the property owner either buys a house at low value and sells it for a much higher value, or buys a house that needs repairs, fixes it up to increase its value and resells it for a profit. This is best utilized when the market is on a downswing. The philosophy behind flipping homes is that if you can make a sale before interest begins to accrue, then you can make big profits. If you really feel that you have it in you to make a business of flipping houses, it is to your advantage to consider a number of options to make it work.

Your first option is to evaluate your cash and assets to determine if you're financially able to take on this endeavor. Assets such as your home, personal savings, retirement accounts, credit cards, and credit lines can be used towards a down payment.

If your credit is in good shape, you can also apply for a loan. There are different types of lenders: banks, private lenders, and hard money lenders.

Consider speaking with your current banker, but keep in mind that traditional bank lenders tend to have higher interest rates. Banks are more likely to lend funds if you can provide a clear lien on the property. A lien is a legal document that states one party has the right to keep possession of property that belongs to someone else until the debt owed is paid. This document is a primary way creditors collect what they are owed.

A private lender is an individual with liquid money that is willing to make a loan with a pre-determined interest rate. Private lenders are more difficult to find, but their interest rates are likely to be lower than banks and hard money lenders.

A hard money lender is a company who borrows money from individuals at one interest rate and loans that money to other private individuals at a higher interest rate.

If these options seem to be too much of a risk for you, it may be worthwhile thinking of forming a partnership because this may give you more funds to play with. If you know people with the right kind of skills, you can discuss how you can make this work for both of you. There are a few things that you need to think about before committing yourself. For example, if you do form a partnership, who is responsible for what? The reason that I say this is because I have seen partnerships go wrong when one person has different ideas, but I have also seen very successful partnerships, where one person is responsible for the work while the other is the investment partner who looks out for property and knows the property market well enough to make good investments. That way, you split the expertise and can each stick to your own specialty.

The other advantage of going into business with someone else is that gives you a potential increase in the amount of funds that you have available to spend on houses. You need to go into this in detail and find out how much you are both prepared to put into the business. If you do this, then you should set up contracts with a lawyer so there is no question or debate down the road about profit sharing or responsibilities of each party. You will need to take out necessary insurance to cover the usual risks during the renovation of a property, but you may be able to get business rates as opposed to individual insurances in the case of a partnership.

When you first make the decision to invest, you need to know your entry and exit costs. Entry costs will include the price of the property, closing costs, repairs and improvements, taxes and insurance while you own it. Upon exit, you will pay closing costs. Please note that if you list with a realtor, your closing costs will also include sales commission. Also, if you borrowed money to finance flipping the house, you will pay interest while you own the property.

Other things that you need to look at are long term investments. If you are flipping houses and find yourself with extra cash, you can consider buying properties that are rentals and increase your potential cash flow. Cash flow is extremely important when you are renovating a house and keeping all the records up to date is essential to ensure that you don't go over budget. A monthly income from a renter could actually pay the mortgage and that's a good investment. If you buy multiple properties, the cash flow is improved and you will be able to use some of the cash coming in for the improvements that you have to make on other properties.

There is a good living to be made from flipping houses, but there are times when the cash flow will be hard to cope with. If you have set up accounts with all of your suppliers, having monthly payments in place may be prudent so that you can keep an eye on exactly what funds are going out at any one time.

If you are prudent with your purchases and always allow enough cash flow to cover the renovations, you can keep this in a bank account that accrues interest so that you are actually making money off of your own money. If you are working on more than one job at a time, you will find that it is beneficial to have arrangements with a team of subcontractors who you can rely upon and move them from one job to another as needed. You will need to keep for your tax records.

Fostering relationships with contractors and with suppliers is essential because this makes you more likely to get bargains along the way. When you see that the budget is stretched, you can also get together with your partner and agree where cuts can be made to bring the projects that you are working on back on track.

If you watch programs like Property Brothers, you will know that this partnership works particularly well and that there is that partnership of skills – organizational and practical – and that's important when it comes to flipping houses. You may even develop such a reputation that you will be able to offer your services to people buying homes so that you refurbish the home using someone else's money but are able to mark up the price so that you turn a profit anyway just by giving that client the benefit of your expertise.

Selling your property

The most basic strategy for selling a home is hiring a real estate agent. You will want to look around for someone that you trust and know can sell your property. Listing agreements give agents the right to earn commission on the sold property and establishes important features of the property and what the price will be. Commission is typically 6% of selling prices for agents and is split 50-50 between the seller's agent and the buyer's agent. There are cases where your agent will also represent the property buyer and be able to keep the whole commission. Real estate agents, the good ones at least, will help you with pricing if you aren't a pro at it. Your agent can look at other properties that are similar and do price comparisons to help you reach the best price.

Real estate agents can take over the showing of your property. To help your property sell, as the seller, you can stage your home with furniture and décor. Talk with your agent, as he or she may have connections to help you with staging. Once an offer is made, the buyer and seller enter negotiations. The two will settle on a price and terms for the sale. A mediator will facilitate the sale by funneling monies and having you sign documentation. Your mediator could be a title and escrow company or an attorney.

While real estate agents can relieve you of some seller duties, you do not need one to sell. With a 6% commission, you are losing a lot of money that you could save by doing the work yourself. The biggest advantage to working with agents is their ability to list on the Multiple Listing Service (MLS). Realtor.com, one of the most popular websites for property browsing, is the home for all MLS property listings. By choosing to sell on your own, you are missing a huge marketing opportunity. But everything else agents handle – putting out a for sale sign, showing the property, networking, posting on other websites, managing negotiations, setting up title and escrow, and handling paperwork – are tasks you can handle. Some agents have begun charging a one-time fee to list a house, but will not do any of the other tasks listed above. If you can find an agent that is willing to accept the flat fee, then you are in great shape for saving on a commission, but still finding viable potential buyers.

After seeing all that goes into selling a property, you may not want to go through the hassle. These are other options for generating cash flow and can prolong your exit on a property.

Chapter 10 – Additional Real Estate Investment Strategies

When investing in real estate, there are a number of ways to generate income. Residential income properties are properties that the owner gains income from. We've already discussed the real estate basics of buying a new home, buying a fixer-upper, as well as flipping. Next, we will take a look at other common real estate investment strategies. Each of these strategies provide its own benefits; however, it is up to you to decide what works best for you.

Buy and Hold

Buy and hold takes the opposite approach of flipping houses. While a house flip is best utilized during a downswing in the economy, buying and holding is great for when the market is improving, and the improvements will last over time. With this strategy, you would buy a house and sell it at a much later date. During this "hold" time, you can rent your property out to tenants. With the buy and hold method, in order to make a profit, the house will need to appreciate in value. Therefore, understand the current real estate market before deciding on this strategy.

Multi-Family

Multi-family property is a lucrative real estate investment. We have only discussed single-family properties up to this point, but by acquiring a building that can hold more than one family, you are opening yourself up to long-term, consistent financial returns. It is important to note that anything over five units will place you into commercial real estate. To avoid that, you should look for properties that have two, three or four units.

Essentially, the rent that tenants in a multi-family unit pay could cover all the expenses for the property and also provide a profit. There is a constant demand for short-term living options. Although you have more turnover with multi-family housing, there will always be a need. Individuals needing a place to live may not be able to save for a down payment, or may be unsure of where they want to settle and need flexibility. For these reasons, making a multi-family investment will expose you to new potential customers.

There are advantages to investing in multi-family properties. Leasing prices in multi-family developments can be adjusted on a daily basis, changing according to the supply of units and demand for those spaces. Multi-family units tend to be owned by individual investors; thus, homes are sometimes closed on quicker than larger properties, the sellers are more flexible, and there is less competition. Large companies and investment groups are going after larger multi-family developments, so by keeping it to four or fewer units, you can have an easier time investing in these properties than with other available investment strategies.

House Hacking

House hacking can be a great way to get started with multi-family rental units. "House hacking" is a term used to when someone buys a multi-family property and lives in one of the units to eliminate costs. Rent from the other tenants would cover the owner's unit as well. For example, if you were to purchase a three-unit home with a $1500 mortgage, you could charge $1000 in rent to each unit for a total of $2000. This would give you a $500 profit after the mortgage is paid.

For most rental properties, you have to put 20% down on the mortgage. However, if you buy as an owner-occupant, your down payment can be decreased to a lower percentage. The owner-occupant status is typically applied to someone who lives in the house for at least a year. With single-family homes, if you buy as an owner-occupant, your ability to expand to multiple properties would slow down. You would live in the home for the first year so that no one would be renting from you. With two to four units, you can begin renting immediately.

While there are many benefits to house hacking, you will have to decide if the lifestyle a multi-family unit would provide to you. Most loans will only require you to live in a unit of your property for one year, but perhaps that is not suitable for you right now. In order to expand, you can continue to enter multi-family building mortgages, but you would move every year.

You also need to consider how much money will you make in your area. Every location is different, as demographics and laws can make a difference on your market. For example, if you are in a college town, multi-family units could provide a constant stream of tenants. However, turnover on your units will be high. On the other hand, if you live in an area where the market wants stability, single-family homes may be a better investment for you. Do your research on your market -- look at what properties are available, as well as supply and demand. Determine what will provide you with the highest return on investment.

Condominiums & Townhomes

Another investment niche is condominiums and townhomes. Condominiums are buildings that have individually-owned apartments. Many condominiums are similar to apartments and townhomes in terms of floorplans; however, ownership is different. If you were to purchase a condominium, you would own the inside of your home, but the exterior and land are owned by an association. With a townhome, you own the land and are responsible for interior and exterior maintenance; however, community amenities are handled by an association.

Single-family and multi-family homes in developments may also have an association to handle community-wide needs. These are typically called homeowner associations (HOA). Established by a community board, the HOA governs a community with a set of rules and spends funds on shared properties, such as a clubhouse, entranceway, and streets and sidewalks. When formed, HOAs establish rules called covenants, conditions, and restrictions. Members of the HOA board set monthly dues for all homeowners and can restrict rights of owners in jointly-owned properties. If you plan on renting, then you will need to make sure your tenant knows all of the HOA rules to avoid any additional fees or charges.

HOAs affect real estate investing, as an HOA can adopt rules that restrict members from renting out units. HOAs also require owners to pay HOA fees. Most do not have an opt-out, as you will benefit from their work. The primary responsibility of HOAs is to provide administrative oversight of gardening, outside repairs, pool upkeep, trash pick-up, snow removal, common areas, and collection of dues. HOA fees for condominiums tend to be higher because HOAs cover repairs of the roof, elevator, exterior walls, walkways and the land itself.

Although the additional fees of an HOA can become costly, it can also be a selling point for some audiences. I remember early on in my career looking at a single-family property that charged $200 a month in HOA fees; however, the HOA offered two 'resident's club' facilities with three swimming pools, two workout facilities, a computer room, dog parks, and playgrounds for children. Although the fees were hefty, tenants were willing to cover the charge because it replaced other costs they may incur, such as gym membership, ink cartridges, entertainment for children, as well as gas to use other facilities.

The cost of buying condominiums and townhomes are often more affordable than single-family or multi-family homes; however, the cost of ownership may be much higher once you consider HOA rules and fees. Additionally, aside from the HOA, there may be other rules enforced throughout the community. One example is that a percentage of units must be occupied by owners, or banks will only approve financing for specific units in a community. Before purchasing any property that is tied to an HOA, be sure to do a holistic financial analysis, as well as background research. You want to make sure your investment is worth it and that you can achieve your business goals.

Vacation Properties

Have you ever vacationed somewhere and thought to yourself, I could live here forever? By investing in vacation rental properties, you can have a second home somewhere you love and visit as often as you'd like while earning income. Earning income on a vacation property would be similar to a rental agreement, in that tenants are paying to occupy the space. The biggest difference will be the length of time they stay. As the owner, you can set criteria for your property. Perhaps you only want to rent Monday through Friday to keep weekends open for you. Or you only do full week rentals. That is all up to you. You can advertise your property on websites like Airbnb and VRBO, which are typically used by individuals seeking safe, affordable rental properties for vacation. There are fees associated with listing on these websites.

Because renters are only staying for a short period of time, you will have higher turnover costs than with a traditional rental. Each time a vacationer uses your property, you will need to pay for a cleaning crew to go through and also fix any damages by the time the next renter comes. With so many people in and out, you may have to fix damages more often. You can charge a refundable deposit to cover any potential damage to your property.

Vacation homes are sometimes in communities, like townhomes and condominiums. You will need to be aware of the rules and any additional fees that may come with renting out your property. The community may charge a usage fee, or may require certain furnishings for your unit. Look into this very closely before signing on the dotted line.

If you are purchasing a vacation home for the added benefit of having a place to stay when you want to get away, then you will want your financials to add up to where you can cover your trips. Vacation rentals are most worth it when they pay for themselves and can cover your vacations as well. Your business plan for your vacation home will need to address all costs, number of rentals per year, and at what rate. Research other rentals in the area to see what they are charging, as well as local hotels. You will want to be competitive in your pricing, but still able to earn a profit. Calculate your return on investment. Before purchasing, be sure to meet with an attorney to draft documentation for your renters to sign. You will want to protect yourself and your property as best you can.

Raw Land

Your investment niche can be even more bare bones than a single-family structure or a condominium. Raw land has the ability to grow into much more. Just like properties, land can be leased or rented. Land can be subdivided and sold for profit. Land can also simply be held onto. With land, you can't create more of it. Many parts of the country are already experiencing issues with land shortages. The need will continue to outweigh supply, which will only make land more valuable in the future.

But if you want a property structure on land you acquire, you will have to develop it. Developed land will generate more income than raw land. Land development is the process of preparing land for construction, including demolition, clearing and grading, rezoning, and installing sewers and utilities, and streets and sidewalks, if necessary. Your team for developing land will differ slightly from your team for existing properties. You will need to hire more subcontractors and perhaps consult additional attorneys to ensure you aren't in violation of any town or city codes.

Rent-to-Own Properties

A rent-to-own or lease agreement is a binding contract that can either allow renters an "option period" of paying rent towards a down payment for the house or requires renters to purchase the home after the lease term. With a lease option, at the end of the option period, the buyer can go through with purchasing the home or not. The option period is usually one to three years, but there is no requirement. If at the end of the option period, the buyer decides they want to own the home, a percentage of the monies collected will go toward the down payment. If the buyer decides they do not want the home, then all monies will be considered rent and given to the seller.

There are benefits for buyers and sellers in rent-to-own agreements. For homeowners, if your home isn't selling fast enough and you're motivated to move out, offering a rent-to-own contract opens your home up to more potential buyers. However, if a new potential buyer makes a higher offer on your home, you can't do anything. Once you enter a contract, you must fulfill your terms. For buyers, a lease agreement is an opportunity to lower debt or save for a down payment, and increase financial stability before taking the leap into homeownership. Before renting, be sure to set your criteria for renters. You can choose to complete a background check on applicants. Ideal residents will have good references, steady source of income and the ability to pay on time. To ensure you have the best tenants, you can also set an income requirement and require a reference check.

An extra step that isn't required, but recommended, is pre-qualifying your renter. This could start an upfront conversation about the feasibility of the renter buying the home at the end of the option period.

If you're worried about losing money with this option, there are ways to protect yourself. If someone is interested in buying the house, but needs a lease option, secure a nonrefundable deposit to go toward the down payment. In your initial agreement, determine the option period. During the option period, a portion of the rent will go towards the down payment. Determine what that percentage will be.

Here's an example: Your house is worth $250,000, and typical rent would be $1,000 a month. Someone who's renting is likely to pay $1,250 a month in rent, with $250 in rent credits. Add a $5,000 nonrefundable deposit, and over three years, the renter will have $14,000 accumulated for a down payment.

Once you have an understanding of a lease-to-own agreement and decide you want to move forward with it, the next step is finding a renter.

1- Do your research. Determine the house values and rental rates for homes nearby. Comparable homes on the market will give you an idea at what price to list your home.

2- Protect yourself. You can buy forms to sell your home via a lease-purchase agreement from US Legal Forms. Outline all aspects of your agreement using these forms to legally protect yourself. Another good practice is to have a mortgage broker or a real estate lawyer take a look at your paperwork and ensure everything is covered. Your agreement should also determine who will cover maintenance, repairs, and home improvements. You will also want to disclose any known issues with the home with your renter.

3- Market your home. There are some online marketplaces that allow you to list your property. Some will charge a fee for listing. You can also use signs to advertise your home is available for lease.

In a rent-to-own agreement, the seller remains the owner and will make any mortgage payments on the property. Terms, interest rate, and the payoff amount will remain intact, despite a new agreement. In some cases, a homeowner can assign the mortgage to another borrower. The third-party is then legally responsible for making payments, and the lender can enforce the lien through foreclosure.

If the shoe is on the other foot and you are interested in being the renter, then it is important to note that if you decide to purchase at the end of the option period, you must secure the financing for the home. Lenders will look at your credit rating, income, savings and what these numbers say about your ability to meet the monthly payments. Market values on houses change all the time. As a result, the original purchase price you received before the option period may be lower or higher than the market reality at the time you're ready to make the purchase.

At the end of the agreement, if the buyer is still unable to qualify for a traditional mortgage, an alternative is wraparound financing. With this agreement, the buyer makes a down payment and signs a promissory note to the seller for the remainder of the purchase price, plus interest. Each month, the buyer will make payments to the seller, and the seller will pay off the existing mortgage. While this financing option will save on closing costs, both parties are more vulnerable, as the buyer must trust that the seller is making mortgage payments, and the seller is reliant on the buyer's monthly payments.

If none of these options look appealing to you, consider starting small and renting a room in your house. Work with an attorney to draft terms of a lease. Everything should be covered in the leasing agreement including lease term, utilities, and potential nuisances. Renting a room doesn't put you in the position of renting out an entire property, but still provides additional income and help in paying expenses.

There is a rule of thumb for investing in property. Let's say your meeting with someone casually and an investment opportunity presents itself, but you don't have your financials right in front of you to determine if its worthy of a conversation. Use the following rules to help you quickly evaluate a property's financials. The numbers will not be exact, but are a good starting point.

The first rule is controversial, mainly due to changes in the real estate market. The 2% rule says that monthly rent should be approximately 2% of the purchase price. The 2% rule is controversial because depending on the market you're renting a home in, the property value may be too high to also meet the average rent for the area. In other words, according to the 2% rule, a $200,000 home should rent for $4,000 a month. The inverse of this rule would be an average three-bedroom home rents for $1,000 a month, so you should look to spend around $50,000 for a property. I will argue that while a $50,000 property meets the 2% rule, it does not take into account repairs that may have to be done to the home or the neighborhood that the home is in. This is where further conversations about the property will help you decide if it's worth evaluating. The 2% rule is driven by cash flow. The closer you are to 2%, the better your cash flow for the property.

New real estate investors sometimes underestimate how much it truly costs to own property. The 50% rule was designed to show expenses are always more than you think. The rule states that 50% of all income received from a property will be spent on expenses, not including the mortgage. The additional expenses are repairs, taxes, utilities, insurance, and turnover costs, including vacancies. If you are charging $1,000 a month in rent, $500 will go towards expenses. If your mortgage payment is $450 a month, then you are receiving $50 a month towards cash flow.

The final rule states that you should only pay 70% of the after repair value less repair costs. For example, if you plan on fixing a home that should sell for $200,000 and needs $20,000 worth of work, then the most you should pay for a property is $120,000. The 70% rule is a quick determination for a maximum price one should pay, but should never be the only calculation used. For this rule, and any listed above, some deals are worthy of a more detailed analysis. When in doubt, take the extra step in evaluating deals.

This book mainly deals with residential real estate investing; however, commercial real estate is also an investment option. Commercial real estate is valued differently than residential property. Commercial properties are valued based on the usable square footage. Properties can be multi-family homes, office space, hotels, retail space, and industrial property. The bulk of money on commercial real estate properties comes from appreciation when it is sold; however, similar to renting a home, you can have tenants use your commercial property.

Commercial Real Estate

Leases on commercial property can range from one to ten years. Multi-family units will have shorter leases while office spaces will be longer. As a rule of thumb, the larger the square footage a tenant is using, the longer the lease can be. There are four different types of leases: gross lease, single-net lease, double-net lease and triple-net lease. With a gross lease, you would collect rent, but are responsible for expenses such as property taxes, insurance, and maintenance. With a single-net lease, tenants will pay property taxes, and rent. With a double-net lease, tenants will pay insurance, property taxes, and rent. With a triple-net lease, tenants will pay maintenance fees, insurance, property taxes, and rent. There is strength in longevity, so you want the best lease agreement that will maximize rent and minimize turnover. Turnover can become expensive for owners as often, a space needs to be adapted to the needs of the tenant in commercial properties. For example, an office space may turn into a dance studio, or a classroom may turn into an office space. Be flexible and willing to negotiate with potential buyers.

To analyze a commercial investment opportunity, evaluate the same criteria you would use for a residential investment: location, the physical condition of the building, zoning and price. Similar to the 2%, 50% and 70% rules discussed earlier, a quick evaluation of commercial properties can be determined by calculating the cap rate. Cap rate is the net operating income (NOI) divided by the offer price. NOI is the net income after all expenses have been paid, except income taxes and debt services). Investment properties sell in the range of 8% to 15%. The higher the cap rate, the riskier the investment. You will want to invest in properties that are in the 8% to 10% range. For a property that will generate an NOI of $10,000 and an offering price of $120,000, the cap rate would be 8%.

Financing commercial real estate differs greatly from residential properties. To finance through a bank, you will need a substantial down payment, typically at least 30% of the final purchase price. Collateral is something you own that provides value to the financer if you are unable to make your payments on the commercial property. You can use private residences and securities. Lenders will want something that is easy to convert to cash, so houses are commonly used as collateral.

Another financing option is balloon loans. With balloon loans, you make interest-only payments during the life of the loan, and then pay the entire amount you originally borrowed at the end of the loan. Balloon loans are risky because you must have the money available to make the balloon payment at the end of your loan, but your monthly payments may be more affordable. If neither of these is viable, you can look at seller financing and partnerships, which are also options for financing residential properties.

Once you finance the property, make an offer. Like residential properties, be sure to do your due diligence and open a title and escrow account. Work closely with your lawyer to review the deal. You will also have to sign a letter of intent about the property and list all contracts involved. Final escrow documents will include a bill of sale, deed, title affidavit and assignment of contracts, warranties and supplier guarantees. Take a detailed look at all of these items to ensure it aligns with everything the seller told you. If anything goes wrong, you have a window of time where you can cancel the escrow transfer.

Commercial real estate investing has its pros and cons. Evaluate your goals and objectives for investing, as well as your resources. Be realistic with the time, money and skills that you have. If goals and resources aren't a factor, then determine which investment niche will yield you the highest profits. Look at how cash flow will differ with residential properties than commercial properties. Determine how much your expenses will be. Also, consider how much time you will spend managing each of the properties. All of these factors will lead you to the best decision for you.

Conclusion

In case I haven't convinced you to begin investing in real estate yet, let's recap significant reasons to enter the market.

1- You build equity. Home equity is an asset that increases financial security for homeowners. With each investment, you are improving your net worth.

2- You will make more out of your investment. The after-tax rate of return on real estate investments far outweigh other investments such as stocks, money market accounts, and CDs.

3- You get tax breaks. With homeownership and real estate investments, comes write-offs including interest, insurance, repairs and maintenance.

4- You can generate your own cash flow. If you choose one of the leasing options, you can have a steady stream of cash flow that can cover your living expenses.

I remember the first house that I bought on a speculative basis. I learned from mistakes and you will too. The thing is that I have used my mistakes to try and set you in the right direction so that you don't make the same mistakes. This is a huge investment that you are about to make, so it's important that you know what you are doing. If you are using the equity in your own home to finance your first house to flip, chances are that you are using the same lender and if this is the case, you may be able to negotiate advantageous terms for that loan. I was able to do this on the first couple of houses and that helped a great deal.

I was able to get great discounts on all of the building materials by letting the builder's merchants know of my intention to go into business. They want your business and the mark up that they use in their sales allows them a little bit of leverage. If they think you will be a regular customer, they will be happy to discount what you buy.

Have lots of catalogs available to cover things such as tiling, work top counters, bathroom fittings, shower fittings and flooring as well as kitchens. These are your mainstay supplies and if you keep yourself up to date with what's available, you will be able to switch suppliers when new lines come out that are more cost advantageous.

Flipping houses may be something that you have always wanted to do and you can do it. You just need to be able to recognize the houses that you should walk away from. If you see unexplained cracks in a house and cannot find the cause, walk away. If you find that floors move as you walk on them, find out why or walk away. If you see electrical installations that are faulty and it's fairly obvious that the wiring is not up to code, check further before you buy. You need to know that all of the costs are under your control at all times and by being careful from the beginning, you really can save money and buy wisely.

As far as code goes, if there is any alteration to be made to the exterior of a home, you need to know that the local planning department is likely to agree to your requests. If you do find that homes are protected because of something historical, beware. These homes may have to be renovated using specific skills to keep their authenticity and may not be the best kind of properties to consider if you are considering moving the property on.

Look out for those deals that come from foreclosures because often the banks only want to make back the original debt, but have them checked out thoroughly before parting with money.

You may have to look up changes to code where there are septic tanks involved as the world is becoming more and more conscious of the environment and septic tank installations are particularly expensive. In rural areas, make allowance for this when you are buying a house. You may find that the cost of bringing the home up to code is excessive. Bear in mind also that people want a home that is a viable proposition from the point of view of economy, so check this out from home owners before you buy. Outdated central heating systems can cost a lot of money to run and may not be viable for the future.

If you follow the advice given in this book and inspect the home from top to bottom before you buy them, you can save yourself a good deal of problems down the line. The roof condition is important. The straightness of the walls is important as is the stability of the foundations. You also need to bear in mind the climatic conditions and the likelihood of flood damage or damage by the weather, particularly in areas where flooding and tornadoes is concerned. Know everything you can know about the property and you will be able to move forward without nasty surprises lurking.

I have been in the business of flipping houses for the past twenty years and have found that I enjoy putting imagination into the renovations that I do. If I can offer potential buyers something that they cannot get elsewhere, then it will have been worth the extra effort. Adding artistic flair to a renovation and really thinking out the space that the house provides helps. If you don't have this expertise, then by all means talk to someone who is good at layouts and décor because the help they can give you may help you to make more money. A friendly architect in your area may become your best ally.

Above all else, read this book through again. The information is there and you need to make a shortlist of all of the things you need to do before you actually go ahead and make an offer. That includes doing background checks on the market that you are aiming for and preparing the house for that market, knowing that the market is vibrant and offers you a chance to give the potential buyers what it is that they are searching for. That's a satisfying feeling and once it happens, you will be spurred on toward the next project and the next because that's what flipping houses is all about. The next challenge is always going to offer even more scope than the last one did. People in this business don't let up. They simply get better and better at doing what they are good at.

Instant Access to Free Book Package!

As a thank you for the purchase of this book, I want to offer you some more material. We collaborate with multiple other authors specializing in various fields. We have best-selling, master writers in history, biographies, DIY projects, home improvement, arts & crafts and much more! **We make a promise to you to deliver at least 4 books a week in different genres, a value of $20-30, for FREE!**

All you need to do is sign up your email here at http://nextstopsuccess.net/freebooks/ to join our Book Club. You will get weekly notification for more free books, courtesy of the First Class Book Club.

As a special thank you, we don't want you to wait until next week for these 4 free books. We want to give you 4 **RIGHT NOW**.

Here's what you will be getting:

1. A fitness book called "BOSU Workout Routine Made Easy!"
2. A book on Jim Rohn, a master life coach: "The Best of Jim Rohn: Lessons for Life Changing Success"
3. A detailed biography on Conan O'Brien, a favorite late night TV show host.
4. A World War 2 Best Selling box set (2 books in 1!): "The Third Reich: Nazi Rise & Fall + World War 2: The Untold Secrets of Nazi Germany".

To get instant access to this free eBook package (a value of $25), and weekly free material, all you need to do is click the link below:

http://nextstopsuccess.net/freebooks/

Add us on Facebook: First Class Book Club